I'M
RISING

ISBN-13: 9780985552718 (eBook)
ISBN-13: 9780985552701

Illustrations by Anna Valenty
Cover Designed by Aleksandra Bilić

I'M RISING

Michelle G. Stradford

Determined. Confident. Powerful.

Also By Michelle G. Stradford

When Love Rises

DEAR READER

I'm Rising is a result of finally letting go of fears and insecurities that prevented me from sharing my growth journey to realizing my potential. Ultimately, it is about self-love and finding and harnessing our strengths and owning our power. Some of us are lucky to be born fearless; others like me had to learn how to become formidable in the face of life's challenges. This second book in my "Rising' series is a culmination of years of capturing my thoughts in journals, on a magnetic word board, or long writing sessions at the screen. I have always turned to writing as a means of sorting through my thoughts and processing whatever life has brought my way. Writing it out was often the only way for me to quiet the noise in my head long enough to get a good night's sleep or to destress at the end of a challenging workday. It has also served as a beautiful form of therapy for when the unthinkable things have occurred in life.

I am grateful to have the opportunity to share my thoughts, words, and ideas with you, so thank you for purchasing and reading my book. My greatest hope is that you will discover meaning and find comfort and inspiration on at least one of these pages. Much of this book was written over the last several years while the Me-Too movement was taking shape. I realized how much frustration I was harboring by not ever having dealt with the personal and professional abuses of power I've experienced. Hearing the agonizing stories being shared unearthed the pain I'd buried, often bringing on tears. It forced me to process my own experiences, understand both the impact and the lessons they offered before I could will myself to move past them.

Now on to something a little lighter. Butterflies are fascinating beautiful creatures that are often used as metaphors for the insistent growth and change experienced as we transform into and rise to what we were meant to become. The symbology of butterflies is something I've connected with all my life, so much so that it is the one and only permanent marking on my body. Thus, you will find images of butterflies used throughout I'm Rising to reinforce the messages of metamorphosis and the capacity to rise that is inherent in each poem and each of us.

DEDICATION

This book is dedicated to my daughters Madison and Camdyn. May you achieve whatever you desire in life as you are both strong, gifted, and fierce. I love you, each beyond measure and words.

TABLE OF CONTENTS

I rise before the sun.
Work to do, places to go
before good fortune comes.
Must stretch this mind,
flex my unflappable,
bat away excuses.
Push way beyond,
all that I ever
could imagine

CHALLENGES

These are my
ordinary moments,
my failures,
heartbreaks,
my joyful messy.
The extraordinary
triumphs,
the real poetic stuff
from life itself.
Take what moves you
leave be the rest.

Joyful Messy

But for all the lies
you spew out
to cement over reality,
blackout my truths,
I'll never stop fighting back
with facts, actualities.
Set straight
your privileged falsities
with veracity.
Rescue my honor,
fragile but unfaltering,
firmly bolstered in certainty.
I channel this hold
you've fixed upon me,
your false sense of supremacy,
the suspicions you propagate,
into metamorphic powers.
Authenticity gives rise to
my unrivaled authority.

Truth to Power

Stunned disbelief,
numb founded my senses.
Though purple patches
bleed through my skin,
I'm frozen over,
can't feel my mouth.
Then my heart pulses a twinge,
releases a hot tear,
switches on the light.
Rushes blood to my head
throbbing, stirring
something inside again.
Crushing pain signals
I'm still alive.
Wound tight with rage,
assaulted but not halted
I stand ready to fight
for my life.

Not Halted

I close my eyes
and catch my demons
crouching in the dim corners
of my consciousness.
They crawl into the crevices
of my laugh lines.
Murmuring of moments
best forgotten,
I blink and turn my head
to shake them off,
try to elude these
unwelcomed stowaways,
who travel inside
of my dark circles.
I patiently await
the arrival of my
cavalry of courage,
so that they can stand
together with me,
to speak witness to
your undoing.

Stowaways

Since you refuse
to understand
my clearly articulated words,
turn and find the door.
No still means no.
Just go.

No Still Means No

I came back
to gather up
my original whole self,
my unyoked wildness
before my zest
was stripped away.
Where free will
was broken out of me.
My badass spirit
beaten down
so that I could be
directed and coaxed
to do your bidding.
Silenced and obedient
while you rode me.
Take note,
I'm back running free,
living loud,
sprinting through life
unbridled and
unbroken.

Unbroken

I'm Rising

I escape the dreamless night,
and smile to brave the day
I have to win this fight,
so, I steel these tears away.

I bathe in healing rain,
fold up fear inside a prayer.
I laugh to numb the pain.
A cure's out there somewhere.

I fuel my soul with song,
dance about on weary feet.
Resolve worn thin, worn long,
for now; I've evaded defeat.

Yet still, I find I fail
to claim the winless prize,
that sets my heart a sail,
re-lights the glow behind my eyes.

Inconclusive test results
is the news just in today.
So, I swallow in resolve
and kneel once more to pray.

Tomorrow I'll brave the day.
Yes, I'll do it all again.
I'll hold despair at bay,
for I have to live for them.

Brave the Day

My obsessively active mind
zooms in and out of clarity
entrapping logic inside
of an impervious pale fog
through which I squint to see
my fingers trembling
as I pull my jacket tighter
to still these body shakes
chilled by cold droplets
diving from my forehead
into a raging river of angst
and throbbing pulsations
that I just can't stop
until I breathe deep
and exhale slowly
then repeat again
and again
until I convert
this agitated energy
into action.
It's over
I'm good.

The Panic

My commitment to
my desired future state
is stronger than
the sweet taste
of this addiction,
a temporary
promise of release.
I pray for strength
to stamp out the seedling
of this unbearable hurt,
to unchain me
from this dependence.

Unchain

Weak and newly wounded,
I swallowed the hurt.
Then cried it into
the salty sea.
I dropped to my knees
sinking into
the crystal sand,
And beseeched the universe
to fix all that
is wrong with me.
Choking back
the pain-filled years,
I lifted praying hands,
as I tasted regret in these tears.
I looked up to see
ripples of the valor
I'd lost rushing back to me.
They swirled about my feet,
fused all my mangled parts
into an artfully mended
undefeated strong
and seasoned heart.

Seasoned Heart

I'm Rising

This dead space,
awkward silence
between us
is the final response
you will ever receive
to your nonsense.
As what you said,
I most certainly take offense.
This icy stare
is with intent to clear up
your confusion, to reset,
offer you space to realize
the impact
and insensitivity
of those words.
The final chance
for you to apologize,
to show some modicum
of respect.

I Take Offense

You stole my natural born,
trusting innocence,
but not my memory of it.
I sealed up the hurt,
now use this unjust
to help others heal.
I work hard
and thrive.
I choose forward.
That is where Life is.

Life is Forward

I have zero tolerance
for those who expect all,
yet offer nothing.
When a NO person enters my life
looking to use me,
exploit my kindness,
challenge my values,
and prey upon my goodness,
I stop them in their tracks.
Swiftly jettison them
to the exit
back door, side, or front.
Just out of my trajectory,
clearing the path for
all the YES people
destined to alter my life
at the prescribed time
that they are needed most,
to share in my journey
to greatness.

Just No

Their sordid smears
fuel my drive.
Bring it.
Keep firing me up!

Fired Up

Make a date
to scream and shout
with your closest confidant,
to vent your frustrations,
life's craziest experiences.
Talk it out.
Hold each other accountable,
to scream louder than each other.
Trying not to laugh
until you collapse together
in uncontrollable hysteria.
Clearing out and releasing
life's toxins.

Release

I'm Rising

You can never heal
that which you forbid
your heart to feel.
While the numbing
to survive is necessary,
pain relief is fleeting,
always temporary,
if you never go
deep enough to
face it directly.

Dig Deeper

These colorful walls
conceal the white lies
that lurk behind thin coats.
We were great at
painting over
the sinister sins,
the dark truths,
alive and breathing
just beneath
the shallow surface.

These Walls

Don't become prey
to negative forces,
predators who slip in,
cling to the deep folds
of your thoughts,
ride your wings,
weigh and drag you down
with every utterance.
At every turn, neutralizes
your next move.
Then lands the
unexpected stinger,
holding their poison
until just the perfect time.
Releasing and twisting
snaking their way
into your psyche.
Pull out and fling away
all and anything
that injects pain,
causes you anguish.
Pluck out and remove
the not easily repelled
from your life, allowing
you to move freely
to excel again.

Pull out the Stingers

These callouses on this soul,
my hardened outer surfaces
thwart destructive words
untold injustices,
from permeating
poisoning all thoughts,
my positive view.
Weakening my faith,
snuffing out the fire
that fuels my heart.
These hard-earned
protections, they shield
prepare me
for life's trials.
This rigid facade I show
was cast from
my experiences
to protect my
essential core.

Rigid Shield

Deliver me through
to the peaceful side
of this painfilled journey.
God, you have granted me
a beautiful life.
Blessed with family
freedom of choice,
material comfort.
You have walked me safely
over, around, and through
obstacles, pain, triumphs.
So, once again I humbly
ask you to help me continue
to believe that with your help
I will beat this thing.
That tumors and illness
cannot destroy what
you have ordained.
Please lead me through this trial.
Forge me into a steadfast,
faithful believer,
a more nurturing mother,
and a supportive wife.
Make me worthy of another
chance at life.

Lead Me Meditation

Storms roll in
to disrupt,
purify,
cleanse,
and restore.
I'll do my part
to prepare for
and adapt to
the impact,
Ready myself
for a transformative
life change.

Life's Storms

Adrift in the breeze,
with no place to land.
Uncertain of what
or who I am.
Holding my breath,
I try hard to shake
this nameless feeling,
a drowning weight.
A wanting, a needing
an aching pain.
Heavy, but hollow
what is this thing?
Thick gray mist shields
the morning light,
hovering low,
blocking my sight.
It draws me near,
then pulls me in,
holding me prisoner
in this place again.

Hours inch past me unaware.
Lost in my thoughts,
I wonder where
to look and search
to find me.
Betrayed by the life
I wanted.
Now from which
I must flee.
From where I stand,
I can almost see
the triumphant victor
I'd planned to be.
Then I hold real still,
and breathe again.
I see my direction
in the power of my pen.

Found My Anchor

Do you measure
the quality of a friendship
by the secrets
they can hold
on whiskey and wine?
Or by the moments
you've enjoyed,
an unprompted laugh,
trust that's long-developed,
over shared travels
and spirited good times?

The Measure of Trust

I refuse to remain
caged and weak,
entrapped inside this anguish,
silly feeble emotion.
I am unassailable,
a hundred times
greater than you.
Break these chains.
I will you to
release me.

Anguished

The stronger and more
self-reliant we appear,
the greater our need
for nurturing,
the taller the longing
for that one day
when our significant
ones feel us,
know when our vibe is off,
and calmly steps in,
taking the helm
and just steers.
Gifting us the
desperately needed pause,
yes, a blank space
where nothing is pending.
That we can never
admit to needing
and refuse to
request of anyone.

Neither dependency
nor reliance come easy
for the driven.
But we will happily accept
the occasional lift.
An offered hand,
the urging to slow our roll.
Despite our disposition,
a tendency to believe
we can achieve
the near improbable.
Invincible, we are not.
Yet without amendment,
we soldier on this journey,
leading, running out in front.
Or cheering,
supporting from behind.
As all that we do
is in the end for them,
those we love,
must protect,
making the whirlwind
we need and thrive in
worthwhile.

The Driven

A woman's body
soon forgets
the intense pain
of giving birth to a new life.
But never can
her heart erase
the indelible ache
of losing her child.

Indelible

   for Virginia, Edna, Tywana, and Joan

I'm Rising

Even the strongest voice
can be misdirected,
persuaded to abandon reason,
ditch deep-rooted beliefs,
doubt their prowess,
themselves,
and join the chorus of lies
that drum loudest.
Project your voice,
stand guard of your
conviction.

Voice Your Conviction

Do not judge or diminish
my struggle because
you believe yours to be
more trying, distressing
or nobler than mine.
Emerging whole from
life-limiting challenges
is not a competition,
I've set out to win.
No, my struggle
is the daily wave I ride
against the tide,
that at once
submerges and
raises me up.
Let us each
be strengthened
by the lessons we've learned,
the wisdom we can
impart to one another.
Not by the relative weight
of the burdens we are
each tasked to carry.

Struggle Worthiness

Michelle G. Stradford

You touched innocent trust,
a budding high spirit
with your wanton fingertips,
teasing them into
a painful frenzy
until you let blood.
Broke in.

Molester

I'm Rising

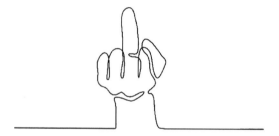

I knew it was okay
to make a bad choice,
take the wrong direction.
But didn't know
how to recognize
the red flags.
I foolishly attributed
the bat he used
to bash in my new car
after a break-up
to not wanting to let me go.
Never realizing
the danger signs
that believing I could
change him,
find the one thing to do,
to fix things between us
had put me on a path
of self-destruction.
I was so caught up
in how deeply
he loved me,
because his passions
ran so high, were needy.
His mostly
light-hearted spirit,
the way he
made me laugh.

I'm Rising

I hid little secrets
from my family,
sugared over the truth,
made excuses.
Exaggerated how great
we were together.
I was ashamed
to tell my friends,
afraid they would judge
both me and him.
After all, I was a smart
young professional,
educated and prepared
for the world,
who didn't know a thing
about how abuse
first eats away
around the edges
of your self-esteem.
Starting with
a backhanded comment
that strips away
layers of you,
your self-worth
day after day.

Followed by the denigration
of your achievements
in a joke designed
and delivered
to lower your value,
an unfounded accusation,
questioning your loyalty.
Putting you on the defense.
A gripping hold
on your wrists today
to prevent you
from leaving the room,
leaves a telling bruise
that your co-worker notices
tomorrow.
But you tell them
you got caught in the door.
Then a crushing slap
in the weeks to come
is soothed by
an apologetic kiss.

After a shove to the floor
next month,
you finally get smart.
You pack to leave
only to be accosted
at the back door,
held hostage by
a night of pleading.
But a promise that there
wouldn't be a next time
ends in broken parts of you,
shattered pieces of me.
Don't repeat
my poor judgment,
and bad choices.
Never put your physical
and mental fitness
in jeopardy.
Leave now
to save you.

Save You

Michelle G. Stradford

The person who
refuses to let you
shake them off
when you'd rather
hideaway,
shut out the world,
stays true even
when they are
the angriest with you,
sits in silence
in your darkest
of moments,
shows they believe in you,
in everything they do,
have etched on our hearts
their vital worth
in permanent markers.

Permanent Marks

Examine the questions
that cause your
pulse to quicken.
The answers you receive
are where
your future lives.

Examine

The truest of friends
show up when
acquaintances judge,
family members
are intolerant,
and the rest of the world
doesn't know
you exist.

Truest

I'm Rising

The stench of rotting ache
sharpens in the
damp dead of night.
Mushrooming into
a suffocating
odor of despair,
multiplying phobias
that go airborne.
It refuses to dissipate
into the bottle of red
that promised to drown tears,
numb the world
if poured into fresh wounds.
Instead, the sting
has intensified.
The miasma of pain
looms larger,
as it tumbles out of the bed
one step behind,
mocking me,
driving a train down
the middle of my head.

Michelle G. Stradford

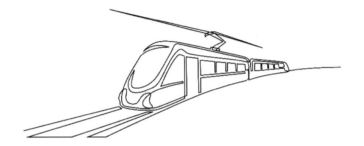

I'm Rising

It twists and tightens
clinging to my new morning,
refusing to release
its' slimy grip
until I open my blinders wide.
Admitting finally
to the lift I need,
the rescue from
these paradoxes inside.
Letting in someone else
in to help me fight,
who's strong enough to pull
me through this listless night,
out into the open
into a fresh view
where the seeds, spores,
the special strain of agony
can no longer survive.
They lay limp, thwarted,
shrinking and dissipating,
finally neutralized.
I hold tight to
this steady beam
of cleansing light.

Neutralized

First, learn to
command respect.
Then request that
those with a different view
from your perspective
give you due reverence.
If they refuse,
explain the choice
of which exit to use.

Choices

*Don't fret when
your first choice
isn't granted.
Second chances
can be your
best path
to achieve greatness.*

Second Chances

Speak up, talk it out.
Give voice to your pain
and say it out loud.
Call out the oppressor.
If you cannot summon
your strength,
trust someone.
Allow them to lead
the way out.
Don't let hope make you stay
in a soul-wrenching place
nor allow anyone
to invalidate you.

Let go of anyone who
is on a mission to
beat down your pride,
or slowly siphons off
your esteem
by making you
the inside joke,
a punching bag,
a personal slave.
When in doubt,
lead with you.
Mind and body
are sure to follow.
Faith and hard work
will see you through.

Lead with You

There comes a time
when we have
little choice but to
confront the aching.
Can no longer be afraid
to stare it in the eyes.
Feel the thrashing
all over again.
Relive the pain,
feeling it lash you
like a thousand
tiny paper cuts,
scraping in slow motion
across your skin.

Aching

I'm roused by
slumbering doubts,
twisting and doubling
me into knots.
Out loud, I scream.
Shout.
Stream hot tears,
and collapse
into a
trembling heap.

Night Terrors

Salty tears sting
my eyes.
Waves of shock,
shake and curl my spine.
In the nanosecond,
she deliberately stepped
onto the payment.
My mind bends,
body forms a rigid board,
bracing for the brake.
My eyes lift
to her, hurtling
thirty feet into the air.
Pain ripples through my core.
Gray matter splatters.
I see blood spewing,
bones snapping,
skinless tissue tearing.
My mouth opens
in a primal scream,
but the knocking
in my chest
explodes and drowns
out my sounds.

I'm Rising

Her gasps gone garbled
into a frozen heap
a listless broken life,
on the shoulder
of a bustling,
and thriving highway,
that leads
to a beach paradise.
My eyes are riveted
on the woman figure
swollen with the promise
of unborn life,
writhing and twisting
to an anguished violent exit
A stranger's face,
her fate seared
into my adolescent psyche.
Forever part of me,
my memory for eternity.
An unforgettable
and preventable
the end.

The End

You are expected
to leave a relationship
that is emotionally
traumatizing
and physically abusive.
Reject any semblance of shame.
Don't wonder what if.
Never accept the blame.
No trying to change them.
Don't second guess
your instinct.
Just go.

Go

I live in urgent motion,
measuring the moments,
gauging them through
a quality of life meter.
A must complete before
it is too late checklist.
In search of a positive effect,
learning or deep moral
that results from
the sum of every
sixty seconds,
the mounting minutes.
Expecting to feel
an impact.
As the precious gift of time
beats on,
counts down,
never-ending,
and slows for no one.

Impact (death of a loved one)

.

Never allow shame,
the concern
of not being believed,
allow you to spend
one longer moment
in harm's way.
Whisper it,
blurt it out.
Scream or write it down.
Unleash your voice.
Release yourself
right now,
today.

Unleash

My thoughts ricochet
back and forth.
I battle for control.
Command them
to move me forward
into the light,
in the right direction.
There is no follow-through
as they refuse to respond
to the unimpassioned.
I am no longer guided
by my own vision.
Rather have allowed forces
not yet understood
steer my life,
halt freedom,
limit progress.
Replace my confidence
with unease.
Reluctant to undertake
a pathway
I know was destined
for me.

Paralyzed

Locked in a
confounded
twisted place,
unable to break
from this paralyzing pace.
Passions pent up,
piled high,
behind a well built
really lit self-constructed
way of life.
Providing for needs
daily comforts.
But freedom.
But happy.
The unattainable
wants.

Prisoner to Comfortable

Feed the hunger
that drives you forward.
When in doubt,
in need of relief,
fill up on
spoonful's of courage.
Never abandon your beliefs.

Spoonful of Courage

Michelle G. Stradford

EVOLVING

Ripping off the scabs
of deep hardened
distorted scars,
skin long thickened
from the repeated
slaps in the face,
I've transformed.
I'm full-grown audacious.
No, I won't be backing down.
Committed to whatever the cause.
Not ashamed of the thorns
in my crown.
No challenge too great.
No obstacle so tall.
I will triumph
just as I have before.
I am a warrior,
after all.

Warrior

If I had my way,
I'd slowly rise on a
lazy July morning,
easing into
this brand-new day.

As if I had no
deadlines
or commitments,
as if I owned my own life.
I'd stretch,
yawn, and stand
in the large
arched window,
and feel.

Squinting in pain
as blinding
white reflections
gleam on the lake below,
fixated,
I'd struggle
to remember.

I'd throw open
the white French doors
to the screened verandah,
losing my breath
momentarily
to the muggy
southern heat.

Easing myself into
Grandmother's
old red rocker,
I'd feel her presence
embrace me,
as a flash of memories
flood my mind.

I'd rise and descend
the worn wooden steps
to the lake below,
reveling in the sounds
of splashing,
and my children's laughter,
If I had my way.

If I Had My Way

Push past your angst,
trample down those
seemingly
insurmountable
obstacles.
Liberate your creativity.
Breakaway from rules.
Level up.
Get there another way.
Celebrate who you are
and become
what you need to be.
Be that one
who just has to
give more,
go at life aggressively
with the highest intensity.
Do the extraordinary.
Be excessive.
Yes, raise the stakes.
Be the bar.
Just live
your life extra.

Live Extra

No matter the cost,
take the detour.
Get hopelessly lost.
And open an unfamiliar door.

Detour

Michelle G. Stradford

I dive deep
and breath life in,
inhaling each obstacle
blocking my path.
I choke out the dark sacs
of vision smothering smoke,
permeating my lungs,
filling me with
soul-sucking layers of soot
until it pours out
of my mouth and nostrils,
blocking out all light,
blinding my path,
disrupting my growth.

Still, I feel
my way forward
and find a hidden
rare pocket,
that one last reserve
of energizing air,
and breathe in the miles.
Then exhale long and wide,
spraying my blaze of fury,
careful not to
char my courage
or trip on regret.
I trample over
old trepidations
now singed into hot ash
from my ire.
I'm a dragon.
I feed on my fire.

My Dragon Fire

Michelle G. Stradford

She rejected all notions
of limitation.
And chose not to see
or hear dark commentary,
criticism of her faults,
never allowing censure
of her thoughts.
For it was her lone raw voice
on the line.
Her skin sauntered down the runway
flourishing in her imperfections,
readily flaunting
her vulnerabilities,
brandishing her imperfect smile.
Half-exposed secrets,
brilliant lights ricocheting
off her toothy flash
for the cameras, the leers.
Commanding all
to regard and acknowledge
the elegant specter she had become,
though had long been for years.
Too tall and proud,
too brash
to be any longer ignored.

Flaunt Your Imperfection

Just once let your
unruly thoughts
run unrestrained
without filters or direction,
overruling your
logical mind,
your stand guard reserve,
protector of
a meticulously ordered life.
Let them lead you
on an exciting uncharted
adventure into
unsuspecting
reckless abandon.
And heart first into
an experience without
purpose.

Unruly

Never allow life's
daily challenges
to shade you gray.
Stay true to the unique
and scintillating you.
Crave your colorful.
Flaunt your vivacious truth.
If ever your rainbow
starts to fade,
remember you are wonderful,
marvelously tailor-made
to just be you,
and to live each day
in your vibrant hue.

Vibrant You

I'm Rising

Amplify your vision
and configure your gifts
into your desired reality.
Hold them up high,
steadfast, and protected,
shouldered on your
relentless tenacity.
Then sound off loud,
belt it out and, be heard.
Yes, amplify yourself.
Keep the volume blasting,
until your dreams are throbbing
incessantly in your head.
Letting you stop at nothing
short of your vision
until you're departed.
Embrace your talent.
Harness your fate.
Live and amplify
your passion.
Don't wait.

Amplify

I'm Rising

My solitude ushers in
unexpected breakthroughs
clarity, creativity,
a little corner of peace,
an over-abundance
of self-reflection.
I celebrate the ability to flow
neurons across both hemispheres
of my consciousness,
to blend ideas,
compose solutions
from the unresolved
heaps of messes
of my life.
Even when it has
led me to analyze too long,
or make self-limiting choices,
I've evolved enough
to allow the world
to intrude on my solitude,
to stretch
and expand me beyond
what I believe
myself possible of.

Ambiversion

Choosing
a reason, a goal,
a passion,
that is unwavering,
charters the pathway
to a successful you.
Owning your conviction
and resolutely focusing
on your purpose
will never allow you to
get lost in the How's
Or cause you
to lose sight of What
is important.
Remain steadfast
in the reasons
that compel you
to show up,
to make a way to be,
to become your
Purpose.
To support your
Why.

Unwavering Why

Define yourself
not by that which
you have become,
but by a measure
of one thousand times
what you believe
you are destined to be.
Constantly re-define
and refine you.
Launch a
You-volution.

You-volution

I will stop
building dreams
only to pull away
the pieces
like a Jenga
then helplessly watch
them crumble
I'm showing up
for Team Me
today and every day
to deposit daily
convictions
one small
accomplishment
at a time

Only I can create,
assemble the framework
for my envisioned reality
by giving two hundred percent
more than is required.
I fortify my capacity,
my drive,
and intellect
with daily servings of faith,
helpings of knowledge
to feed this dream,
keep it alive,
and advancing forward.
I remain alert.
Prepared to construct
a rock-solid plan.

Dream Strong

I test critical ties
for strains and kinks.
I rely on them
to hold me firm
in my convictions,
make me stronger than
I would be,
If I chose to walk alone.
Though they may bind,
tighten, bring discomfort,
Allowing them
to carelessly loosen
or stretch thin, and taut,
will result in
irreparable breaks
in my spirit.

Vital Bonds

So much more moves me
than they will ever see.
A tapestry of incongruent
inconsistencies.
More than potential,
I'm a juxtaposition.
Soft velvet,
hardened wood,
a shiny steel fabric
heartened by life,
weaved and fashioned
into the rarest human art.
At times rigid,
or warm and malleable
when I need to be.
I'm a force.
Pure mettle.
Built and made solid.

Layer upon layers
of colorful character,
rich in hidden talents.
These untapped dimensions,
delicately stitched together
with threads of apprehension,
a unicorn's moxie,
untold multiplicities.
Made reliable and flexible,
readily transformable
into anything.
Evolving.
Becoming everything.
Yes, all that
I've ever wanted to be.

My Multiplicities

I'm Rising

The serenity of the sea
intoxicates, coerces me.
The rhythmic roar undeniably
at once frightens and soothes.
Ahh excites me,
pulling me under its current.
This incubator of life heals,
restores my will to try,
brings clarity to what I've seen.
It casts a spell,
teaching me to accept
my plurality.
Holding me forever near,
I crave the feel of its flow,
over and through every pore.
Cleansing and restoring.
As much a part of me
as my reason for being.
Here, I'm never alone,
giving me the sanctity of mind.
This natural oasis
keeps me strong.
This sea feeds me.
Is me.
I'm owned.

Owned

The day she learned
her truth was invaluable,
that she could achieve great things
without changing who she was,
that woman tailored her talents.
Polished her flaws,
packaged them both up
as treasures of wisdom to live by.

Industrious

I inhale language,
voraciously
craving lessons of wisdom
from my favorite books.
I journal my neurotic thoughts,
working out the hard learned
youthful knocks,
the growing pains.
Practicing the mindfulness
of the older,
and would be wiser me,
I pour myself a cup of kindness
and whisper positive
affirmations as a reminder
of my evolving soul.
Prayerful of a kinder heart.

I am grateful each day
to embark
upon a renewal journey.
A fresh start,
I drink in moments,
my elixir goes down
languid and slow.
It will be my way
in due time.
In the clarity of morning
I map out my path for the day,
and in the morrow,
designing a masterplan
for the sweet nectar of life.
As I wait,
yes anticipate
a positive overflow.

Morning Joe Flow

Lay your blanket
beneath the folds
of the stellar velvet night,
and listen close
to the melodies played
by the stars.
Those strewn far
and lighting our milky way.
Tune in to you,
learn something new,
Find inspiration in the
messages the universe
has just for you
Get lifted.
Be moved by the pulsations,
hear the fiery plasmas
crush against
your gravitational pull.
Let the sounds fill you,
seduce and lull you,
as each star
plays its' own
galactic concerto song.

Star Songs

Excuses and successes,
whether a noir or blue day.
Unreasonable expectations,
is it a must-do or may?
One relies on inaction,
the other work harder,
less play.
My unwavering action,
a well-thought strategy,
is what got me here.
Astute and promising prodigy,
where I now aim my sights.
Sacrifice and a touch
of genius are key.
I decide how to get it right,
it's all up to me.
I am my own advocate,
the Chairman, and C.O.D,
Chief Officer of my Destiny.

Chief Officer of Destiny

I blasted through
the fire blazed wall.
Cracks here and there,
no evident breaks
Risked it all.
Even through the shakes,
I willed me free.
Now flying, soaring,
I am finally whole.
Freed my spirit
and drove a stake
thru the demon's soul.
Jumped feet first
into this hardened world,
with no lifelines left.
I'm in control.
Newly intrepid,
I'm a survivor.
High on confidence,
I own this new life.

New Life

I hold my hand
for a long moment
beneath the rush
of warm water,
as rising heat
steams the room,
tingling
and flushing my face.
Beaming in the
balmy comfort,
I light yellow flames
that flicker
in excited anticipation.
Fatigued feet,
cooled on Spanish tile,
carry me
to catch the lock.
As soft saxophone notes
waft, sway and still
my frayed mind.

While lavender oil
free-falls
from the crystal vase,
that I pour
from high above
the white claw-foot tub.
Where
purple puddles
gather atop
the gurgling waters,
awaiting
the commencement.
I close
these weary eyes
and submerge
my worries
into the liquid
sanctum.
Dissolving away
the pain,
and filling up
on promise,
until I am
restored again.

Purple Sanctum

I'm Rising

All I have
are these
unique life experiences
to share.
All I know is that
my infrequent,
audacious,
adventuresome moments
revolutionized me,
while I was unaware.

All I Know

Night falls heavy
upon us
to restore our bodies,
reset the rhythms,
point us back
in our intended direction,
so that we don't
outrun the day,
break time.
Shut out your worries.
Turn off the lights,
and slumber well.
Take care of yourself,
Regenerate your life cell.
Prioritize you,
go renew.

Renew

Swallowing hard
to hold anxiety in check,
feeds its growth,
not mine.
I opened my mouth
and regurgitated
the colony of lies,
that lined my gut.

Gut Check

She relished a day
when she could
halt time,
still her pace,
find mindful motionless,
go sojourn,
saunter in tranquility.
But she could only
downshift into
a sprint,
a time-lapsed blur,
because goals
won't achieve,
transform life,
without her
furious.

Furious

Treasure that you
have experienced
enough to overcome.
Celebrate that you
have thrived thus far.

Love every inch and ounce
of your exquisite woman.
Embrace the awkward
girl you once were.

Love all that you
have become,
the trailblazer you are
evolving into.
Your imperfections.
Your sins and scars.

Even when you
are not your best,
shower adoration daily
upon yourself.

Love Mantra

The death of my demons
commenced the moment
a ray of morning hope
filtered through
the interminable dark.

My fortitude finally awoke,
opened these shutters,
and ushered in
the cleansing light.

Open the Shutters

Is anything truly original?
A newly birthed human.
A rare flower.
This never yet lived
but perfect hour?
Yes, each part of you
is a rarity,
an original new,
gone in an instant,
never to be repeated moment
waiting for you
to generate
a magnificently tattered
perfect fabric of you.

Original New

I'm Rising

I drink thirstily
from this life spring,
source of inspiration.
Words are spewing
from this well
of wistful thoughts.
Memorable babblings
burst forth.
From the experiences
of the lived,
loved and lost,
m version of life.
I live to write words,
this reading of my heart
out loud,
is my remedy.

Inspiration

Commitment
and patience
gestate dreams that
both frighten and inspire.
Don't abort them
at conception.

Nurture

Accepting less than
the intended outcome
isn't falling short,
or lowering your standards.
It's a calming mechanism,
temporary refraction,
a speed bump,
to help you gain
stronger traction.
Slow your mind down
to reassess and recommit.
To help you get
shit done right,
the first time around.

Intended Outcome

When driving hard,
the push to move forward
takes me on a wrong turn,
a mistake sends me spiraling down
an "I told you so" hole.
I remember the sacrifices,
the determined persistence of my forebearers.
I hear their voices urging me to get over it.
Just make another choice
to go around or over,
whatever the obstacle.
I keep going harder
day in and day out,
even when I feel lost and distraught.
Because my insane visions cannot
reach their highest heights,
without me piping in the sweat,
the work, staying in the fight.
To frame this dream and earn the clout,
to become all that I can.
I'll keep going
harder and higher
until I see the last light,
in the moments before my eyelids
are forever closed tight.

Keep Going Higher

Do not once allow
those most essential
to your well-being
to ever question
that they matter.
Never assume,
tell them incessantly.

They Matter

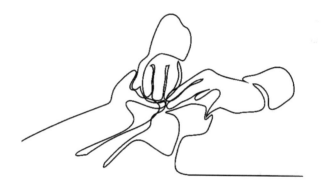

My insistent army
of sharp-witted
commanding words,
clamored through the fissures
of my shattered armor,
shouting urgent reminders
of my sovereign roar.
Screaming out,
I own this!

Adrenalin Moves Me

I steer clear of other
people's assessments
of my intentions,
accomplishments,
my worth.
I turn down the volume
on these outside voices,
so I can hear
the chatter in my head.
And understand with clarity
my own convictions,
my perception of the me
that I aspire to be.
I celebrate and accept
my flaws, my failures
and all those
not yet discovered,
personal treasures.
I value me.

I Value Me

Sharpen your resolve.
Charge forward hard.
Pierce the chamber
that contains your distress,
brings on nervousness.
Then capture the breakthrough,
that's intended for you.

Go Conquer

I pay homage
to every special friend
who has shaped me,
impacted my life
in great and small ways.
Made the moments magical
with a knowing smile,
a caring gesture.
Heaped on unabashed
praise and appreciation.
Or called BS when
I was not giving
my best, most
authentic me.

You Shaped

Entangle yourself
in people circles,
open and translucent.
Link and connect them,
and feel their energy rings
ripple across
genders and generations.
Connect cultures.
Celebrate differences.
Expand beyond geographies.
Travel in circles
that provide a safe,
and accessible place,
that teach tolerance,
supports and inspires you.
Never eclipses
your light.

Circles

Sitting by the edge
of my river of thoughts,
just east of my dream state,
I wade through
my unconscious stream
of gurgling moments.
Those juxtaposed thoughts,
my weary mind,
struggles to make sense,
in search of insight,
waiting to uncover a hidden,
unresolved obstruction,
a treasure,
of breakout disruptions,
certain to reveal
a new lane
I never knew was open
to my ordinary life.

Mapping New Lanes

I move through
rearview mirrors,
slipping in and out of them.
Observing life from
both sides of the glass,
at all angles,
even the edges.
Watching my mind
navigate dimensions of time,
seeing my being
breakthrough all of the
layers of lies.
I'm coming to terms
with who I am,
what still could be.
Finally, I face
that which
cannot be seen
nor understood
head-on.

Rear View

I held up the glass
in front of me,
and caught an old
reflection of the
younger fiercer me.
Hello to my
unrestrained used to be.
Stop trying to grow up so fast
Slow down and give
lots of smiles away.
Ones that are
purposeful and bright,
as if they were your last
chance to make an impact,
set things right.
Pack all the fun
you can in today.
Don't hide your love
like precious art.
Keep it on display.
Grow it profusely,
and give it freely away.
Those with an
open and teachable heart,
learn invaluable lessons
along life's way.

Self-Reflections

Ties that last,
the ones that
forge or shape,
are minted
one shared experience
at a time.
Showing up,
just staying present
merge all the years
into immortal memories,
unbreakable ties,
lasting connections.

Lasting Ties

She was bowled over,
knocked down.
Didn't see
the rocks hurtling,
aiming for her.
Lost supporters,
fake friends,
struggled, stumbled.
Constant kicks to her knees,
suffered the injustice,
threw frozen pity parties.
Obsessed over
what was no more.
Wallowed in red wine
until she could no longer
stand for it,
defend her excuses.
Refusing to live
this way anymore,
she picked up
her confidence,
trusted her instinct.

Chose a new path
over material gain.
Sacrificed stability
for freedom of choice.
With a plan,
relentless effort,
a few positive breaks,
the tide started to turn.
She regained her stride,
used her gift to motivate,
attained all her goals.
No, she could never quit.
Inspired others,
both small and great.
Lifted herself up high,
on the only
thing that remained.
All she had left
was raw grit.

Raw Grit

Michelle G. Stradford

If I could live again,
I'd spend a few hundred years
peering through
wide-eyed lenses,
devoid of pain,
oblivious to tears.
Paint my world with ribbons
in rousing red bursts
of morning sun.
Where anything is possible
no limitations,
not even one.
I'd carve up the day in slices
of freedom from inhibitions,
laughing louder than anyone.
I wake from this daydream
hear the thunderous message,
the needed change,
my recurring theme,
understand what I'm missing.
I must find a better way to live.
Acknowledgment is a power,
is everything.
It is transformative.

Acknowledge

Breathe life
into your dreams.
Try them on.
Check that they are
a size or two larger than you,
not quite a fit,
leaving room
to develop, grow into.
Respond to the requirements
they have of you.
Let them consume
all regions of your brain,
thoughts, ideas.
Live in your dream,
walk around inside them
as if they already exist,
are your new reality,
have already come to past.
If you remain unchallenged,
up the stakes.
Manifest you into largess,
a brilliant success.

Manifest

Stop waiting
for brilliance to strike.
Create a recipe for success.
Show up for you every day
at the same time and place.
Bring your unique talents.
Mix in your inner creative,
and just stir.
Let the magic
of you pour.

Just Stir

Be a standout.
Hold and defend
your position.
Stop lurking in the shadows.
Put yourself out there.
Create a happening,
cause an international incident.
Do something crazy,
some off-color outtakes,
Fresh ideas are crafted
from bold mistakes.

Bold Mistakes

We strong-willed
cease looking for approval
from friends, strangers, all others.
We rely on the innate strength
yes, the unconditional kind
that's baked into our bones
by our fathers and mothers.
Those who held us up,
close and steady,
reinforced principles,
required goals,
supported and protected
until we were ready,
and committed to self-care.
Had self-direction,
understood self-love.
How to cherish ourselves,
just as our kin
had devotedly done.
Now fortified with faith,
drawing on the fire from within.
Raising ourselves up daily
to elevate and honor
the deep lineage built,
long sustained
on strong-willed self-love.

Strong-Willed Love

When your
inner voice
goes silent.
Fill those
conversation lulls
with positive
messaging,
and affirmations
of devoted
self-respect.

Affirm

Keep your circle tight.
They are your fall back,
the place you will always belong.
Draw your people in close
to make you better,
keep you strong.

Keep Them Close

Travel far and wide
to unheard-of places.
Leap at experiences that
test and sharpen your mind.
Makes you better,
different,
keeps your heart open.
Stay close to the people
who ground you in humility.
Accept tough feedback,
the kind that changes,
and invigorates you.
Walk away from your average.
Peel off that thin skin.
Toughen your tenacity.
Attack life like a savage.

Live Savage

Open-up and expose
your vulnerabilities
through circumspect,
a healthy dose
of self-reflection.
They often reveal a need
you never knew
you harbored.

Open Up

Speak your high ambitions
into existence.
Sear them into
your imagined reality
so, they remain constant,
unavoidable in the realm
of your semi-conscious,
as you speed through
the unremarkable,
this life of tedium.
Write them out
to keep you stimulated
enough to escape
the clutches of the inevitable
nightmare scenarios,
making their way
into your head each day.
Stand guard of your creative.
Clear out the daily influx
of should not,
the cannot excuses,
replacing them with why not,
and well planned how to's
that drive your
ambitions forward.
Reach higher.

High Ambition

Slow your pace.
Lose direction,
step off the track.
Explore your other
dimensions,
the ones you've
been discounting.
Find you.
Step out of and away
from that person
you've been
packaging yourself as.
Peel away other peoples'
layers of wrapping
you have acquired
along the way.
Reach and touch
the real.
Feel you.

Take a walk inside.
Look around and focus,
and truly see.
Pause and reflect.
Get comfortable with
the stuck, the messy,
your ever-changing parts.
See and examine you.
Then find your way back,
or create a new path.
Either way,
you are on track,
when you connect
all your magnificence
with the changing parts.
Accept you.

See You Accept You

Michelle G. Stradford

RISING

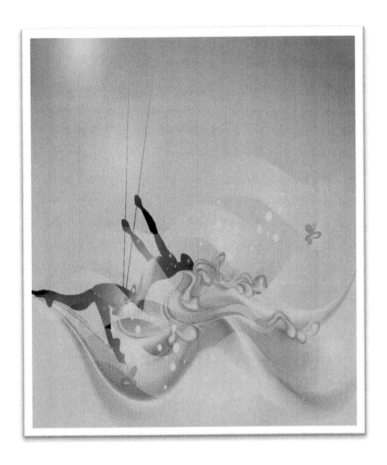

Not holding back
is new for me.
Loving my quirks,
embracing my crazy
has emboldened me.
I'll never again
be that
invisible she.
Yeah, I'm really
feeling this decidedly,
remarkable me.
Recite in the mirror
and repeat.
I got this.
Hello, New She.

The New She (or He)

No more.
No shame.
Step away, fear.
No holding me back.
It's way past time.
This is my year.
I'm taking my power back.
Fed up and frustrated,
I'm standing up.
Done making amends,
I'm here to represent,
lead the debate,
face the attacks lose, or win.
I'm putting it all out there,
giving it my best.
Can't throttle this fire.
Turning up full force,
no time for rest.
Going hard,
sounding off loud.
Worn down and stretched thin,
this is about making me proud.
I no longer rely on hope.
I'm far from defenseless,
I am the revolt.

The Revolt

I was broken
and tired of hiding,
when finally
I held up the mirror
to peer at my
fractured parts,
and saw that
pain and struggle
had not twisted me
into something angry,
unrecognizable,
and hideous.
But into a courageous,
bolder, and more
formidable me.

Formidable

I surround myself in
vast open oceans
of translucent time.

Blazing streams
of liquid moments
rush into my empty well.

I embrace change
and accept life's
course correction.

Laughing down broken
yesterdays, I search for
truth in tomorrow.

I cup my hands
and drink up life,
until I thirst no more.

I devour today as if
it's the end
of the universe.

Course Correction

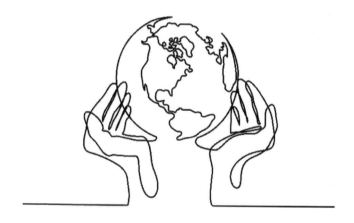

Shield yourself from
other people's misery,
soul-sucking negative energy,
by mixing up a spirited
cocktail of fun,
a bright blend
of your smile,
day filled with sun,
a dose of hope,
trusted family member
or a friend.
Then fill yourself up
with light.
Don't drink from the hype.
Make your own batch
of sunshine.
And go set
the world right.

Batch of Sunshine

Wild and untethered
passion
thrives in deeply
rooted
self-love.
Plant positive seeds.
Nurture and grow
the beautifully made you.

Self-Love

I refuse to become
entangled
inside of these
twisted dark vines,
others attempt to
deep root,
plant in my mind.
Nor allow self-doubt
to grow unchecked
and invasive.
Crowding out my light,
wilting my imaginings
into limp, dried out
possibilities
crackling beneath
the weight of
disquietude.

This naive mask,
I must remove.
Smash the spectacle
of the falsehoods
that I hide behind,
to more easily discern
friend from foe,
be in the know,
that they have my back.
I'll let the leap
in my heart
not the noise
in my head
run wild,
free,
and pervasive.

Pervasive

I am the sum of
my mother's faith,
my father's strength,
God's grace, and
my own determination.
I make no apologies.
I offer no excuses.
Fierce and unstoppable,
I AM
My Superpower.

Superpower

I'm Rising

Facing the truth
fused together
my fissures,
burnished and branded,
these thickened scars
into a hardened fortress.
I'm rebuilt for conquering.

I'm Rebuilt

Cultivate a different
friendship each day,
and share at the
communal well
to keep it
consistently rising,
overflowing with wisdom,
deep knowledge.
Drink thirstily
and fill up on
the strength
you find there.

Communal Wisdom

I own this beautiful,
my glorious,
the way I came to be.
Birthed into this world
to live out my story.
No longer trying to
curate an altered image,
fit into someone else's shoe,
Become an appendage,
a mirror, not ever.
These hips swerve wide.
Curvy mounds boast
proudly from my chest.
Teeth not quite straight,
yet my smile
torches the night.
Natural hair all curlicue,
my luster shines from within.
Even if I never realize,
all I was meant to attain,
I will never again
feel I can't be me,
not measure up.
I am more than enough.

Loving every bit
you see
of the parts I readily share,
and those I keep
just for me.
At times there's a bit
less or more to see,
in places where I
never used to be.
But, I still bet on,
will always believe in me.
I stake claim to
both the inside and out.
My glorious,
my natural born
beautiful bounty.

My Glorious

My liveliest visions
are conceived
with a fresh mind,
right after being kissed
by the morning sunrise.
It's how I cultivate my crazy,
blend new and old experiences.
Meld memories and mazes
with pieces of truths
into intriguing places,
imagined stories
painted onto new faces.
I quench this thirsty,
the need to create
in the light
of first morning,
where inspiration awaits.

Sunrise Visions

Speak with
confidence.
Live boldly,
people,
no matter
how young or old.
Honor your worth,
and set wild ass goals.
Walk proud in your truth.
Yes, rescue yourself.
Make your own happy after.
Free your swagger.
Go ahead and take it.
Own your power.

Free Your Swagger

When hurt jumped on me,
making my tears flow
unexpectedly,
I had to go back
and visit pain where it lived,
to confront the reason
that it still existed.
I found it,
analyzed it,
then beat it down,
stripping it of all authority.
And then added it to
my proud badge of scars,
now the highlight
of my collection of strengths.
Instead of the cowering
weakness that it once was.
Then I went out and celebrated,
the newly minted and thriving,
hurt conquering me.
Mission completed.

Mission Me

I'm Rising

I wager my hopes,
deep passions,
limitless future,
in delirious surrender
to stay in love with life.
For where is the wisdom
in holding-back
me and my talents
from the universe,
since she is free to revoke
them all at will anyway?
I place my chips on the table.
Stake it all
for these positive vibes,
to stay lit on
this electric current,
flowing through me,
for the opportunity to
truly feel alive.
This is my one chance,
my one life,
I'm wagering it all.

Wager

Michelle G. Stradford

She flexed her
stunning energy field,
sweeping up the steadfast ones
into her whirlwind,
ripping apart their
proclaimed
self-righteous
sense of entitlement,
and reset the seats
at the table.

She-nado

Take a pause.
Look around
and enjoy the view.
Amazing things
are transpiring
right there
inside of you.

View of You

I rise-up each day
to claim my daily
source of light,
my rousing energy
from **God**,
the cosmos.
I envision the life I need
to make me feel alive.
I create a plan for all
that I must do
to restore,
generate me anew.
I pray for wisdom,
the forte
to make good choices
in all I do.
To remain present,
I will say I love you
more times today
than yesterday.
I commit to smile more readily,
take the time to appreciate
someone new.
I will find a unique way
to make at least one
positive impact every day.

Rousing Risings

She scripted
the life she
wanted,
working tirelessly
harnessing her brilliance,
to attain her goals.
No handouts
or set quotas.
Done with
mansplaining.
Just doing
her version
of carving out
a gilded living.

Scripted

To you, this drive
appears maddening.
The state of sleep-deprived,
surely unsustainable.
This non-stop energy,
the need to move,
to do.
Quest to be more,
to reach my attainable,
to achieve all I believe
is possible.
I must thrive now
in this chaotic rhythm,
while I'm inspired,
feel unstoppable.
I'll seek harmony in death.
Go at your own pace.
If you can't keep up,
get your rest.
See you in the last stretch,
or at the end of the race.

My Race, My Pace

Warm, happy noises
from my bouquet
of friends' voices
lift up my spirits,
as I prepare for the arrival
of an assortment
of purple, yellow and red
personalities.
Bright faces smiling,
crystal wine glasses clinging.
Vigorous debating,
just stimulating.

West Chester Book Club

I'm Rising

Permit yourself
to live truly free
to exercise the privileges
of the remarkable woman
you were born to be.
Express sexual prowess.
Be your provocative self.
Exert the confident,
the self-assured you.
Be brash and arrogant.
Just take charge.
Attain elite athletic perfection.
Revel in your natural beauty,
or go glam and elegant.
Yes, boast your sarcastic wit.
Be a reckoning,
the boss of your life.
Don't overthink it.
Just do
the unapologetic you.

Unapologetic

She healed
her emotional wounds
by replaying the day
in her head.
Then one by one,
invalidated each rejection.
Sashaying around the room,
to soothing pulses of jazz
until she collapsed,
rippling in
private pleasure.

Self-care

Michelle G. Stradford

I love you
my sweet friend,
because your eyes
dance with
excitement to see me,
as readily as they do
the passerby on the street.
You inspire me with
your open and generous heart,
and the ease with which
you put others first.
Quietly administering
your compassion,
while confidently
and loudly sharing
free-flowing advice.
Spreading your
fierce passion for life.
Energizing us all
with your contagion.
Lighting us up with
the brightest of smiles.
Lucky that I am
to call you, friend.
You are both the silver
and the gold standard.

Make New Friends

Sometimes you must
surrender to faith.
And trust
that you believe in
the right things.
Hold fast to the conviction
of your cerebral
reasoning.
Embrace your
intuitive instinct.
Commit to your decisions,
even when the most
reliable of confidants
give you their back,
disagree and
turns the tide against you.

Trust in You

Some call them
the extended kin.
They stabilize my center,
are my healing balm,
I delight in
their juxtaposed blend
of chaotic energy.
An undercurrent of quiet calm,
only here do I find
constancy, and comfort.
Always at home in my skin.

Gatherings

Sun burnished
Cameroon skin
cover these
Native American bones.
European heritage
flows in the crimson blood
feeding the sinewy muscle,
once riddled with bullets,
whipped by cowhide,
then strung up
and drained of life.
This ancestral concoction
fuels the determination,
stoic fortitude,
that survived bondage,
withstood rape,
inhumane slaughter,
fought for freedom.

Spawned brilliant
inventions.
solutions to problems,
despite the spurn,
burden of disdain
as the face of the lowest
rung of society.
Still moved generations
upwards, forward.
Why is it that you believe
harsh words, ridicule,
division, organized action,
brutality could lessen,
dismiss my intensity,
diminish the evolution,
this mix of great global nations,
origin of majestic ethnicities,
full potency, top blend,
my strong
persistent strain
of DNA.

Special Blended DNA

Beneath the surface
of her tranquility,
that tall and quiet charm,
beat the heart
of an independent
goal slaying
fierce highflying go-getter.
Out of her way.
She trounces the weak,
and flings away
the hangers-on.

Fierce

I'm Rising

Take a long look inside
and feel proud
of the astonishing force
that is you.
Revel in your cache,
the lacing together
of all the intricate layers.
From oldest to new,
both your painful,
most beautiful realities
make up the intriguing being
you've grown into.
The funny smart articulate,
the introspective introvert,
fun-loving flirt.
All the failures, sweet successes,
a shameful moment
some social awkwardness.
The sleepless puffy eyes,
hard-earned lessons,
those laugh lines.
The confident glow
all spell out the story
of sublime growth,
the elegant
strength of you.

Elegant Cache

I rendezvous with
the stripped-down
version of me
in the clarity before dawn.
There in the quiescent still,
I face and reckon with
the unfiltered,
the raw and teachable me.
I arrive early to meet up
with my maker.
Pray for serenity,
Inspiration,
the capacity, guts to do
something meaningful,
and contribute to the world.
I show up to harness
this feeling again and again.
These are the instants
when I believe
most in myself,
that I can do anything.
I thrive because
these moments
fulfill me.

Me Moments

Each time I dip my pen
into the ink well,
I dig a little deeper
into my resolve bank
and pull up
a new color of delight.
I paint an exciting path
along this journey
of discovering
then letting go
of my self-limiting beliefs,
so that I can make space
for the boundless dreams,
and near-impossible goals,
I am certain to reach.

Mining the Future

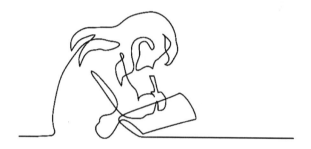

You are the ones
who cover me.
Where I am valued
for the best
and worst of me.
Where my secrets
are protected
and dreams supported.
My bohemian quirks
are celebrated.
I'm held up when I stumble.
The food tastes better,
the drink enriches
our chatter,
and I can dance
my heart out,
when my triumphs
are cheered.
I'm called out
when required.
This is where
I've behaved the silliest,
hurt the deepest.
Yes, cried freely,
the ugliest.

And laughed
the hardest.
There is care enough
to confront,
work through conflicts,
detangle inevitable
disagreements.
You push me to rise
to whatever the challenge,
teaching me that no matter
I will never be left behind
by my kin.
Or truest friends.
We'll walk side by side,
hands clasped
through the end.
My uplifting tribes
move me forward,
push for higher.
Because they
stand with me,
I not only survive,
I thrive.

My Tribes

Michelle G. Stradford

A run alone to reflect,
before the hint of sun
is the closest
I have ever come
to euphoric peace.
That place to belong,
a restoring sanctuary
of my own.

Euphoric Restoration

I'm Rising

I love the way our lives
remain entwined as we have
grown, changed and refined
from fresh-faced
youthful friends,
to valiant, unabashed
skillful take-charge women.
Cheering each other
over the years,
sharing confidences,
silly grins,
Talking each other
through the tears.

I'm Rising

Now raising kids of our own,
I am immensely proud
of your accomplishments,
as much as you are of mine.
You've always seen
the best in,
expected the most from me.
Refusing to let any crap
unnerve, unravel
or allow life's challenges
to break me.
Today I celebrate you
my fearless Sheroe.

Sheroes

Liftoff in
a roaring blaze,
brighter than
anything they
have ever seen,
soaring higher than
you've ever dreamed.
Let them inhale
the haze, the heat
from your burn off.
Blind them in
your light,
your intensity.
Stay on fire.

Intensity

Resilience is a
duel edged, failure based
innate energy,
driving me through
improbable life forces.
Propelling me past my
impossibly poor choices.
Lessening the brutal impact
of my tall fails.
Protecting me from
catastrophic falls.
Forging me into a resistance,
strong enough
to withstand any force.
I continue to press,
test my hand at life,
and will fail often,
but build
my resilience.

Resilience

She longed to soar,
higher still,
accomplish more.
Transport herself,
transform the world
on iron wings.
Built for life's brutal forces,
its' turbulent wind shear,
already tested,
untethered without fear.
So, she left the comfort,
the easy,
the known.
Took the hard leap,
and grew some.

Iron Wings

I'm Rising

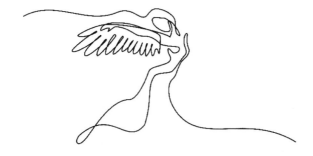

Resolve is taking rise
from this fiery storm,
that's been building.
It's breaking me free
from old crippling fears.
I stand tall.
Stare life firmly in the eye.
Hold my head up strong
and own
this reckoning force,
that is roaring,
loud and resolute
inside of me.
I'm Rising.

I'm Rising

I'm Rising

FROM THE AUTHOR

Thank you for reading my book. I sincerely hope that you enjoyed it and found the words and messages impactful and applicable to your life experiences.

Feedback, whether a phrase, a brief sentence, or a paragraph, is valued and appreciated. It all helps me become a better writer. So, please take a moment to leave a rating and review online at the retailer site where you purchased the book.

To stay updated on my next book release, read samples of work in progress, etc., please connect with me as follows:

Instagram @michellestradfordauthor
Twitter @mgstradford
Facebook @michellestradfordauthor
Pinterest @michellestradfordauthor
Bookbub: michelle-g-stradford
Goodreads: Michelle G Stradford

ACKNOWLEDGMENTS

I thank God for the life experiences that have culminated in this latest collection of stories and prose. Special appreciation goes out to my husband for his support and love over the years, but especially in these last several months of my journey as an author. You are my center and caretaker with a quieting calm that makes me believe I can do anything. I am also grateful for the continued encouragement from family and friends, but most especially my siblings.

To my mentors, too numerous to name, your examples and accomplishments, both great and small, encourage me to work harder and smarter. Because of you, I have opened my heart and life just a little wider, allowing me the benefit of meeting amazing people and achieving the growth I never knew was possible.

Michelle G. Stradford

ABOUT THE AUTHOR

Michelle G. Stradford is a creator and lover of the written word and the visual arts. She enjoys sharing her unique view of the world and life experiences through creative writing. Michelle also thrives when using words, art, and photography to tell stories that evoke emotions or make connections with others. In addition to poetry, she dabbles in short stories and hopes to craft a novel someday. Michelle is married and has two daughters.

"When Love Rises" is the first of multiple books planned in her "Rising" series. It is a poetry collection about life that celebrates love, offers comfort in heartbreak and inspiration to heal, move forward, and try love again.

Look for release updates for upcoming collections in her poetry series, "Rise Unstoppable" and "We All Rise."

Michelle G. Stradford

Made in the USA
Columbia, SC
11 November 2020